# Methodist United Reformed Church Worship:

## Baptism and Communion in two 'Free' Churches

by

**David Kennedy**

*Tutor in Liturgy, The Queen's College, Birmingham*

and

**Phillip Tovey**

*Team Vicar St. Francis LEP, Banbury*

GROVE BOOKS LIMITED
Bramcote Nottingham NG9 3DS

## CONTENTS





**THE COVER PICTURE**
is by David Hopkin

*First Impression* January 1992
**ISSN** 0305-3067
**ISBN** 1 85174 200 X

# 1. INTRODUCTION

It is sometimes salutary to think of what might have been. Had the Covenanting for Unity proposals of the early 80s found sufficient acceptance among the participating Churches, one of the fruits of the scheme must surely have been the production of common liturgical texts. It would have been an exciting process. As it is, the want of a sufficient majority then in General Synod has meant that we have all had to go our own way; and for Churches like the Methodist Church and the United Reformed Church, this has involved a consolidation of their own identities. For the United Reformed Church part of this process has involved the publication of a new *Service Book* in 1989 (to replace the 1980 *A Book of Services*) and a new hymnal *Rejoice and Sing* (1991). The Methodist Church has also produced a new hymn book *Hymns and Psalms* (1983) in conjunction with other Free Churches in Britain and Ireland, and the next stage of Methodist liturgical revision has begun with the presentation to Conference in 1991 of new baptism and confirmation texts. The Methodist Church intends to replace the *Methodist Service Book* of 1975 during this decade. On a local level, much fresh thinking about the nature of worship has been stimulated by the Report *Let the People Worship* (1988) advocating the setting up of local worship consultations.

This booklet is an introduction, from an Anglican perspective, to the traditions associated with the celebration of the sacraments in Methodism and the URC. The Methodist Church of Great Britain was formed by the union of various Methodists groupings such as the Wesleyans and the Primitives in 1932. The United Reformed Church began as the union of the Presbyterian Church of England and the Congregational Church in England and Wales in 1972, to which was added the Reformed Association of the Churches of Christ in 1981. Like the Church of England, the Methodist Church and the URC embrace distinctive historical traditions, and so accept diverse approaches to the Sacraments.

In one sense there is an irony in a booklet about baptism and communion in the Methodist and the United Reformed Churches. This is because in the Free Church tradition the main diet of worship for a congregation is decidedly *non-sacramental*. In Methodism, it is the Preaching Service that is central to its piety and identity.[1] While Holy Communion is more frequently celebrated in parts of Methodism than it used to be, nevertheless, the comparatively small number of ordained ministers in relation to the number of worship centres means that on average, a monthly celebration of the sacrament would be the norm. Indeed, it is likely that many Methodist worshippers would resist more frequent communions even if they could obtain access to them.

While the title *The Preaching Service* is not used in the United Reformed Church, nevertheless, the Sunday worship in that Church is normally non-sacramental, with perhaps a monthly celebration of the communion. Both Churches continue to place great emphasis on preaching and employ

[1] See Adrian Burdon, *The Preaching Service—The Glory of the Methodists*, (Alcuin/GROW Joint Liturgical Study 17, 1991).

the gifts of local or lay preachers to service the circuits and churches. While both churches may make provision for lay presidency at the eucharist, concerns for church order restrict this to exceptional circumstances. This does not mean that the communion is unimportant; indeed, Reformed commentators often assert that, by restricting the number of celebrations and preparing carefully for them, their Churches underline the awesomeness of the occasion and the celebration of the grace of God. Baptism, of course, cannot be discussed in terms of centrality as it is an unrepeated rite, although the generally agreed principle that baptism should be administered during public worship means that there is a greater baptismal consciousness on the part of regular worshippers than in previous generations.

This booklet does not intend to undermine or marginalize the place of the service of the word. It is, however, in sacramental theology and practice that many of the sharp issues separating the Churches find their focus. Moreover, ecumenical sharing and co-operation continues, especially on the local level in LEPs, local covenants, and councils of Churches. We hope that this booklet will outline some of those sharp areas, many of which are also debated internally within Anglicanism.

Throughout the booklet, we have had to make reference to liturgical texts. This is dangerous, because the Free Churches historically have cherished the tradition of free and extempore prayer and have defended their freedoms in contra-distinction to the more prescriptive approach of Anglicanism. Indeed, the URC *Service Book* goes so far as to say, 'the Reformed tradition continues to reject *as a denial of the nature of Christian worship* the imposition of fixed forms of service' (p.vi). The service books set norms and, as authorized documents, we trust that they reflect something of the mind of the Churches. Some Methodist congregations do use *The Methodist Service Book* as a 'pew book'; for some, it is a 'ministerial manual'; for others, it is totally peripheral. It is somewhat rare to find copies of the URC *Service Book* in the hands of a congregation; it is far more a resource for the minister, although texts are included in the new hymn book.

## 2. BAPTISM AND CONFIRMATION IN METHODISM

A. BAPTISM

Christian initiation has been a major area of discussion within Methodism in recent years. It has formed part of the agenda of the annual Methodist Conference in 1982, 1985, 1987, 1988, 1990, and 1991. The 1987 Conference recommended a revision of the 1975 services and new texts were duly presented in 1990. Such was the reaction to these new texts that it was decided that further work needed to be done. Revised texts were therefore presented to the 1991 Conference in Bolton and authorized for use. They have the status of services alternative to those in *The Methodist Service Book*. As the *MSB* itself is being revised, the 1991 services are likely to undergo further revision for the publication of the new book or books. As the 1991 texts represent the most recent Methodist thinking, they will be used as the basis for this chapter.

The 1991 texts provide four orders of service:

1. The Baptism of those able to answer for themselves, with the Public Recognition and Confirmation of Full Members.
2. The Baptism of Young Children.
3. A combination of 1 and 2.
4. Public Recognition and Confirmation of Full Members—as a separate service.

The order of the services is itself significant. The 1975 *MSB* placed infant baptism as the first and therefore normative rite. The new services follow the *ASB* in giving primary place to those who can answer for themselves, doubtless reflecting the Church's grasp of its missionary role in the last decade of the twentieth century.

The General Directions for the services also reveal significant developments in thought when compared to 1975.

**1. Mode and place of baptism.**

The 1975 services instructed that baptism should be administered by pouring or sprinkling or dipping. It was Wesley who added 'sprinkling' as a third mode of baptism in his '*Abridgement*' of *The Book of Common Prayer* prepared for America in 1784. The 1991 rites state that while sprinkling is sufficient, it is more fitting to dip or to pour; this reflects ancient and ecumenical custom. Baptism is no longer confined to a font; direction 4 mentions the possibility of being baptized in a baptistry, river, lake or the sea. Clearly, baptism by total immersion (i.e. submersion) is in business in the Methodist Church and this is to be welcomed.

A triple administration of water is also commended to accompany the Trinitarian formula, although a single administration is acceptable.

**2. Baptismal Discipline.**
The directions state that instruction shall be given to all baptismal candidates or to the parents/guardians of young children before the sacrament is administered, and that normally baptism should be administered at a service of public worship.

This echoes 1975. However, the directions concerning the baptism of children go on to state that where the parent(s) or guardian(s) cannot make the promises contained in the service, then baptism may be deferred. This is a long way from the opening words of the General Directions for the 1975 Baptism of Infants service: 'A solemn obligation rests upon parents to present their children to Christ in Baptism.' The promises in the new service are introduced with the words:

> Dear friends in Christ, young children are baptized on the understanding that they will be brought up in the fellowship of Christ's Church and taught the Christian faith; and with prayer that they will confess Christ as Lord, enter into the fullness of the Church's life, share in the Communion of the Lord's Supper and serve Christ in the world.

The phrase 'baptized on the understanding that . . .' echoes the introduction to the *ASB* service. While the new Methodist rite avoids the explicit statement 'you must answer for yourselves and for this child', the interrogation of the parents is more stringent than in the Anglican service. This will give some encouragement to those Methodist ministers who wish to exercise some discrimination in the presentation of infants.

A table on page 7 opposite sets out the structural character of the rites. There are a number of points of interest in comparison with the corresponding Anglican services:

**1. The Decision**
This triple interrogation is a direct lift from *ASB*, but occurs only in the first rite as a personal statement of faith for candidates able to answer for themselves. In the case of young children, the parents are asked to promise that they will bring the child up as a Christian and declare the faith of the Church in the Apostles' Creed, but there is no suggestion of faith by proxy. Whereas the *ASB* is careful to separate the Decision from the Profession of Faith, regarding the former as preliminary and reflecting the more primitive order of the rite, the new Methodist rite follows the 1662 Prayer Book structure by running them together.

**2. The Thanksgiving over the Water**
Baptism as a water rite is given greater prominence in the 1991 services than those of 1975. The baptismal prayer of 1975 is essentially a thanksgiving for redemption, followed by four petitions for fruitful reception of the sacrament. The prayer includes no water imagery, still less any sense that the water is blessed or set apart. In the *ASB* there is the explicit request 'Bless this water' and this troubles some evangelical consciences, though the blessing is 'that your servants who are washed in it may be made one with Christ . . .' i.e. the blessing is conferred in the administration.

## THE STRUCTURE OF THE BAPTISMAL RITES

| **Those able to answer for themselves** | **Young Children** |
|---|---|
| *The Preparation* | *The Preparation* |
| Hymn | Any part of the Preparation from the Sunday Service |
| Collect | |
| *The Ministry of the Word* | *The Ministry of the Word* |
| (Old Testament lesson) | |
| Epistle | Lessons of the day |
| Hymn | |
| Gospel | |
| Sermon | Sermon |
| Hymn | Hymn |
| *The Declaration* | *The Declaration* |
| Exhortation | Exhortation |
| *The Thanksgiving over the Water* | *The Thanksgiving over the Water* |
| Water is poured into the font | Water is poured into the font |
| Thanksgiving prayer | Thanksgiving prayer |
| *The Decision, the Promises and the Profession of Faith* | *The Decision, the Promises and the Profession of Faith* |
| Interrogation of congregation | Exhortation |
| Triple interrogation of candidates | Interrogation of congregation |
| Triple profession of faith | Interrogation of parents |
| (Testimony) | (Interrogation of godparents) |
| | Triple profession of faith |
| Desire for baptism | Desire for baptism |
| | Naming |
| | (Statement of God's favour) |
| *The Baptism* | *The Baptism* |
| Administration of water | Administration of water |
| | Signing with the cross |
| | Showing of child to congregation |
| | (Hymn) |
| | Aaronic blessing |
| | (Giving of a candle) |
| *The Confirmation and reception* | *The Peace* |
| *The Lord's Supper* | *The Prayers* |

The new Methodist services instruct the minister to pour the water into the font (if a font is being used) in the sight of the congregation, and the new prayer with its rich water imagery is a welcome restoration to the rite, especially in view of the fact that Wesley retained the version of Luther's *Flood Prayer* with its water imagery in his '*Abridgement*' of the *BCP*. The encouragement in the service for a triple administration strengthens further the basic water symbolism. The 1991 prayer still includes no blessing of the water, in the light of traditional Methodist reluctance to bless inanimate objects. However, there is a rubric permitting the minister to stretch *her/his* hands over the water; an epicletic gesture which may betray an intention to confer a blessing, although the prayer is about the candidates rather than the water:

> Look now in love upon your Church,
> and grant that *these* your *servants*,

*(The Minister may extend her/his hands over the water)*

> now to be baptized in this water,
> may die to sin, be raised up to new life in Christ,
> and be born again from above by the power of the Holy Spirit.

The prayer includes a helpful feminine image:

> 'Through the waters of the womb, in pain and in joy, you bring new life into the world'.

**3. Secondary symbolism**

It will be noticed that the secondary symbols of making the sign of the cross and the optional presentation of a lighted candle appear only in the rite for young children. This is probably for the sake of simplicity. There is no provision for baptismal anointing, although Acts 10.38 is alluded to in the thanksgiving over the water. Anointing as a ceremony is foreign to Methodist piety; and there is also the recurring question of whether such symbolism 'speaks' in our particular culture. Concerns about male and military language surface in the traditional words at the signing; 'soldier' is omitted and the text reads:

> By Baptism we receive N into the congregation of Christ's flock, and we pray that *she/he* may not be ashamed to hold fast the faith of Christ crucified, to fight against evil, and to persevere as Christ's faithful *servant* to *her/his* life's end. **Amen**

**4. Baptismal theology.**

Historically, the most distinctive difference between Anglican and Methodist baptismal liturgy concerns the question of realistic language. This can be traced back to John Wesley's deletion of the phrase, 'Seeing now, dearly beloved brethren, that this child is regenerate' in his '*Abridgement*'. In fact, Wesley's views on baptismal regeneration are a cause of much disagreement and debate.[1] While it seems clear that Wesley did believe in the baptismal regeneration of infants[2], his baptismal theology can only be understood in the light of his utter conviction that what matters is growth in grace throughout a Christian's life; the emphasis must fall not on what has happened in the past, but on the reality of a relationship with God in the present. If this is true, then his deletion of the references to regeneration in the Prayer Book was not so much because he disagreed with the words, but that the declaratory statements were misleading as they stood, they were insufficient on their own, and so were better eliminated. Methodism traditionally has fallen shy of 'realistic' language and thus of anything that suggests baptismal regeneration in the case of infants. This is well illustrated in the 1975 initiation services where emphasis falls on growth rather more than on categorical

[1] See 'The Significance of Baptism for the Christian Life: Wesley's Pattern of Christian Initiation' by Henry H. Knight III, in *Worship*, Volume 63, No 2, (March 1969).

[2] See R. E. Davies, *History of the Methodist Church in Great Britain I*, (Epworth Press, 1965) p.160.

statements about what baptism has effected. The 1975 infant rite is also agnostic about the role of the Holy Spirit in baptism, whereas the rite for those able to answer for themselves asserts that the candidate is baptized into Christ's body the church by the power of the Holy Spirit. It is difficult to escape a suspicion that we are dealing with two theologies of baptism according to the age of the candidates. The Church of England has refused to go down this path; identical statements are made both for believers and infants. One of the reasons that the 1990 texts were sent back to the Faith and Order Committee for further work was because of a fear of misunderstanding about realist language in the baptism of infant children. The original text of the Declaration read:

> Brothers and sisters in Christ:
> through baptism, by the power of the Holy Spirit,
> Christian believers and their children
> are made members of God's family, the Church.
> Sharing in the new covenant of God's love,
> they die to sin, are buried with Christ,
> and are raised with him to eternal life.

In the revised texts, the first three lines are amended to:

> Brothers and sisters in Christ,
> through grace,
> through the sign and seal of baptism,
> and through the power of the Holy Spirit
> we become God's people, the Church.
> Sharing in the . . .

The revision seeks to set baptism in a wider context as a means, but not necessarily the only means, of becoming part of the people of God.

At the giving of the candle, the candidate is assured:

> N, you have passed from darkness to light.

This also was singled out for criticism in amendments given to the 1990 Conference on the basis that it could imply baptismal regeneration, but has survived. The difficulty is that if this, argument is taken to its logical conclusion, *very little* can be said about baptism theologically. Certainly, any realist biblical language (of which there is plenty) would have to be omitted leaving us with the question in what sense this relates to biblical practice at all. Of course, some would argue that infant baptism doesn't!

Another interesting feature of the young children's rite is the inclusion of a text based on a prayer from the French Reformed Church. Immediately before the baptism, the Minister says:

> N,
> for you Jesus Christ has come,
> has lived, has suffered;
> for you he endured the agony of Gethsemane
> and the darkness of Calvary;
> for you he has uttered the cry, 'It is accomplished!'
> For you he has triumphed over death;
> for you he prays at God's right hand;
> all for you, little child,
> even though you do not know it.
> In your baptism, the word of the apostle is fulfilled:
> 'We love, because God first loved us'.

This underlines the stress on prevenient grace that is such a pillar of the Methodist rationale for the baptism of young children. The French rite makes the theme of God's initiative explicit by performing the baptism before the parents have to make any promises about Christian upbringing. Therefore, the whole theological context is different and how this relates to the weighty pre-baptismal interrogations of the Methodist rite is unclear!

### 5. Personal Testimony

The opportunity for personal testimony, albeit optional, in the service for those able to answer for themselves is welcome (the URC confirmation service makes similar provision). Coming immediately before the baptism, it rather isolates the common profession of faith made by all the candidates (if there be more than one) and so breaks up the intimate biblical association between profession and administration. After the Decision might have been a happier position.

## B. CONFIRMATION

The full title is 'The Public Recognition and Confirmation of Full Members'. Methodism, with its roots as a Society within the established Church, has retained up till now the language of 'full membership'. This jars somewhat with the theological principle that it is baptism that confers (full!) membership of Christ's Church, and a Faith and Order Working Party on ecclesiology is currently looking at this issue. 'Public Recognition' comes from the rule that candidates for full membership are first accepted as Members in Training and undergo a probationary period of not less than three months before the Church Pastoral Committee recommends them for full membership, and this is publicly recognized in confirmation. The rite therefore has a dual role; part of it is linked with baptism as an act of the universal church; part of it is concerned with membership of a particular local church. Confirmation is a service of strengthening:

> strengthen them now in faith by the Holy Spirit, the Spirit of wisdom and understanding, etc.

This is in line with the theology of the Prayer Book. It is also intended to be seen as an act of positive commissioning for service in the church, although this does not come out as clearly in the text as it might have done. It is noteworthy that Wesley rejected confirmation in his American provision as the Scriptural warrant for the rite is weak. There is some wisdom in this for, where 'believer's baptism' is administered, there is the question of whether any further post-baptismal ceremony regarded as essential for Christian Initiation is necessary. The report on Initiation accepted at the 1987 Conference declared:

> 'We must emphasize that Church membership begins at Baptism whatever the age of administration. Another ceremony will be needed at the time when personal commitment is made and the baptized are of an age to undertake definite responsibilities and offices in the Christian Community; but Baptism is the sufficient act of Christian Initiation and signifies, along with its other meanings, entry into membership of the Church Universal.'

While this justifies a second rite for those baptized in infancy, it remains unclear why confirmation is required for those whose personal commitment is in baptism because they are able to answer for themselves.'

[1] See D. R. Holeton (ed) *Christian Initiation in the Anglican Communion,* (Grove Worship Series 118, 1991).

## 3. BAPTISM AND CONFIRMATION IN THE URC

A. BAPTISM

**1 Structure**

The URC baptismal liturgy follows the structure of historic Reformed rites.

1. Introduction
2. The Promises
3. The Baptismal Prayer
4. The Baptism
5. Prayer

The 1989 *Service Book* has taken account of the inclusion of the Churches of Christ into the union with a 'believer's baptism' tradition. This has been done by having one service with parallel columns for believers and infants. The simplicity of the rite has its roots in sixteenth century Geneva.

Calvin's reformation of the baptism was based upon a number of principles. Firstly, all secondary symbolism was to be removed. He described secondary symbolism as 'theatrical pomp, which dazzles the eyes of the simple, and dulls their minds.' Secondly, baptism was to occur in the main service of the day. Thirdly, it was only to be performed by ministers of the Gospel. Fourthly the theology of the 'covenant of grace' sealed in the old covenant in circumcision and in the new in baptism, led to the abolition of any idea of faith in the child. Children who were to be baptized were done so because they had Christian parents who promised to bring them up in the faith.

The liturgies that ensued were varied but at their simplest were composed of long (and tedious) exhortations, followed by the questioning of the parents' intention to bring the child up in the faith, immediately followed with the baptism. Indeed infant baptism became the normative rite; there was for example no liturgical provision for the baptism of adults in the Church of Scotland until 1874.

The Puritans had developed a concept of consecration. So the *Westminster Directory* talks of:

> 'Prayer . . . to be joyned with the word of Institution, for sanctifying the Water to this spiritual use.'[1]

This would later be developed in Presbyterian rites to an epiclesis on the water. The *Directory* also allowed for the 'sprinckling' of the water on the child, a mode not formally allowed in Anglican rites.

This gives some background to the simplicity of the structure. Now it is possible to look at various issues raised by the URC services and contrast them with the Church of England.

**2 Faith and the child**

The URC rites place the emphasis totally on the faith and promises of the parents and congregation. In the section called the promises, the parents

[1] *The Westminster Directory*, (Grove Liturgical Study no 21, Grove Books, 1980) p.20

are asked whether they believe in the triune God. Then a series of promises are asked for, whether the parents, sponsors, and congregation will all play their respective parts in bringing up the child in the Christian faith. The children of Christian parents 'are within the covenant and belong to the life of the Church'.

By contrast the *ASB* both in the decision and in the baptismal declaration of faith asks that the parents (and the godparents) answer 'for yourselves and for these children'. This rests on an idea of proxy faith. The parents are expressing the faith of the child, in the same way as they have to make many other decisions for their children.

The practice of Christendom was the baptism of infants; adult baptism became very rare. But the tradition continued that the parents provided the faith necessary to receive the sacrament. At the Reformation the Church of England kept this theory. Bucer attacked the 1549 Prayer book on this point.[1] The Puritans sustained similar objections.

The Reformed tradition took a different approach with the theory of the covenant of grace still found in the URC *Service Book*. But if covenant of grace was expressed firstly by the covenant sign of circumcision and then by baptism, what are the differences between the old and new covenant signs? If circumcision and baptism are too closely identified, then baptism may become an ethnic rite, as circumcision was. The need for profession of faith in Jesus is one of the distinctions between the old and new covenants. This is in danger of being obscured when infants are baptized without any reference to their need for faith. The situation becomes acute when adults and infants are baptized in one service.

Both the *Service Book* and the *ASB* try to formulate a baptismal service that is for both adults and infants. In the *ASB* the same questions are asked of the candidates. In the case of children the sponsors answer on their behalf. In the *Service Book* different questions have to be asked of the adult candidates from those asked of the parents; and the URC does not question children. Parents are asked if they will bring them up in faith. Thus, although there is a unified service of baptism on the page, the parallel columns of promises express two sacramental theologies. Children automatically receive grace through baptism because of birth in a Christian family. Adults, irrespective of parents, have to profess faith before they may receive the sacrament. Perhaps Cranmer was correct in resisting Bucer who wanted the Church of England to travel down this reformed route.

## 3 The Baptismal Prayer

Prayer over the water was omitted from many Reformed rites. This may be for a variety of reasons. Firstly, the medieval practice was of an infrequent blessing of the font and the use of pre-sanctified water at baptism. Thus the experience of many people would not be of any prayer over the water at the time of baptism. Secondly, many Reformers were very hostile to any suggestion of superstition in regard to the water and thus abolished blessing fonts, replacing it with exhortations to teach true baptismal doctrine.

[1] E. C. Whitaker, *Martin Bucer and the Book of Common Prayer*, (Alcuin Club Collection no 55, SPCK, 1974), pp.94-96.

Although the *Westminster Directory* hints at the possibility of a prayer for the sanctifying of the water, there are different strands in the Reformed tradition. Some have no prayer at all, baptism follows immediately after the profession of the faith of the parents. Others have a prayer for the effectual working of the sacrament but with no reference to the water. The Presbyterians however developed the hint of the *Directory* that the water is to be sanctified and now include various forms of epiclesis.

*The Book of Common Order (1979)* of the Church of Scotland asks:

> Send forth thy Holy Spirit, O God, to sanctify us all and to bless this water that *this child* may be born anew of water and the Holy Spirit . . .

As such, the Presbyterian tradition stands closer to the Anglican *ASB:*

> Bless this water, that your servants who are washed in it may be made one with Christ in his death and resurrection. Send your Holy Spirit upon them to bring them to new birth . . .

Here is a point of convergence between Anglicans and Presbyterians.

The 1662 *BCP* contrasts with modern rites. In the phrases 'by the Baptism of thy well-beloved Son Jesus Christ, in the river Jordan, didst sanctify Water to the mystical washing away of sin', and 'whose . . . Son Jesus Christ, for the forgiveness of our sins, did shed out of his most precious side both water and blood' a different approach is seen. Bucer was of course unhappy with similar phrases in the 1549 book. But these phrases connect us with some very ancient baptismal theology no longer in contemporary rites. The *BCP* 'Sanctify this Water to the mystical washing away of sin' is a modification of the prayer over the font of 1549. Later the *Westminster Directory* also saw the logic of a prayer setting aside the water as a part of the baptismal act.

The URC books of 1980 and 1989 have included a Baptismal Prayer, indeed they include two alternative prayers. Both of the 1980 prayers say:

> Be with us in the power of your Spirit and so use this water and our obedience to Christ that N . . . whom we baptize in your Name may receive the fulness of your grace . . .

This seems to be the result of a strong Congregationalist influence on the liturgy. The first prayer in the 1989 rite contains an epiclesis but on the candidate:

> Send your Holy Spirit upon A . . . for new birth in the family of your Church . . .

Thus the URC is more cautious over an epiclesis on the water in the baptismal prayer than the Anglicans and Presbyterians.

**4 Secondary Symbolism**

Anglicans have always defended secondary symbolism at baptism, not least the signing with the cross, which the Puritans found objectionable. The *ASB* has increased the range of symbols to include the giving of a candle, and anointing is allowed both at the signing with the cross and at confirmation.

Calvin described exorcism, the taper and chrism as 'this adventitious farrago'. But Bucer almost justifies the signs of the white robe and chrism. He said that as mothers show many outward signs of their love to their children, so these signs, excited the saints of old to greater love and devotion. This is a concession to his usual rather cerebral approach to symbols, and a realisation that symbols should be attractive at a gut level. However he sees humanity's innate impiety as having turned them to 'abominable spectacles' and his fear of superstition leads to his recommending their abolition. Thus the reformed tradition has often only allowed the biblical Aaronic blessing as a secondary symbol (e.g. 1980 book p.47).

The 1989 book introduces the possibility of the giving of a lighted candle, the accompanying wording being very similar to the *ASB*. This is a surprising inclusion in the light of the traditional hostility to such symbolism. Also the ecumenical outlook of the church might have pointed to other symbols. BEM hoped for the recovery of vivid signs in association with the gift of the Spirit in baptism. It looks in particular for the sign of the cross, laying on of hands, and anointing.[1] As the cross was such a contentious point in the past and the laying on of hands occurs at confirmation, one might have expected a stronger element of symbolism of the Spirit to have been included. This is not achieved with the candle.

Some today regard anointing as a 'dumb ceremony' but, if BEM is to be followed, Bucer may point the way forward. 'With the help of some teaching the wholesome use of these signs might be restored.' The Reformers had no objection to secondary symbolism, provided they did not obscure the primary symbol and were not objects of superstition. Is the lighted candle a vivid sign that will help deepen baptismal spirituality? This seems doubtful. But, of course, the same questions could be raised about its inclusion in the *ASB*.

B. CONFIRMATION

Confirmation in the URC occurs immediately after baptism for those baptised as adults. There are separate services for those who were unable to make their own profession of faith at baptism. The structure is as follows.

| **A Book of Services 1980** | **Service Book 1989** |
|---|---|
| Introduction | Introduction |
| | Act of Witness |
| The Promises | The Renewal of Baptismal Promises |
| Prayer | |
| The Confirmation and Reception | The Confirmation |
| | The Welcome |
| Prayer | |

There are a number of differences between the two books. Firstly elders are now allowed to join in the laying on of hands. Secondly the prayers

[1] See B. D. Spinks, 'Vivid Signs of the Gift of the Spirit?', in *Worship*, Vol 60, no 4, pp.232f.

have changed. The 1980 book had an optative subjunctive prayer over each candidate 'The God of all grace . . . confirm and strengthen you' and a performative statement 'I declare you to be admitted'. The 1989 book brings back an allusion to Isaiah 11.2 and is more epicletic, 'send your Holy Spirit upon *him/her/them*'. The new book also makes space for personal testimony from the candidates. Perhaps this option could be included in the Church of England.

Looking at the 1989 book we see some strange features in confirmation. Firstly it is not clear as to why there should be any confirmation for those who have been baptized as adults. If the candidate has received the Holy Spirit in baptism, as is asked in the first baptismal prayer, why have confirmation at all? As in the *ASB*, it seems unnecessary and unclear as to its purpose.

Secondly the relationship between baptism and membership seems confusing. At baptism, it is declared that 'A . . . has been received into the household of God, the only, holy, catholic, and apostolic Church'. The introduction to the confirmation service says 'in baptism we are welcomed into the family and household of God . . . *ABC* . . . come(s) now to make their own profession of Christian faith, and to accept the responsibilities and privileges of membership'. At the welcome is said 'I declare you to be admitted to the full privileges and responsibilities of membership of the . . . Church'. In trying to avoid dividing baptism and membership, the book avoids saying that one becomes a member of the church at baptism. Full privileges and responsibilities are undefined, but the welcome makes it clear that the Church Meeting has to vote for you to be admitted to them. Baptism is not automatically entitlementto such membership. Initiation therefore still remains a two-stage process, baptism completed by confirmation. This may not be something that the URC wishes to say, but it is debatable if the 1989 book has avoided it. The URC, like the Anglican, seems to be in a confused position over confirmation, if for different reasons.

## 4. HOLY COMMUNION IN METHODISM

### Authorized Services

The most influential factor in the celebration of the holy communion in Methodism in the last twenty years has undoubtedly been *The Methodist Service Book*. Neil Dixon describes its impact as 'immense', bringing to the Connexion insights from the Liturgical Movement, a united approach to word and sacrament and the promotion of more frequent celebrations.[1] While the *MSB* is by no means the only starting point for a consideration of Communion, its influence has been formative.

The 1975 *Methodist Service Book* includes two orders for holy communion. The first is *The Sunday Service,* a modern language service first published in booklet form in 1968 and the second is the 1936 order, *The Lord's Supper or Holy Communion* based on *The Book of Common Prayer*. The forms of service in *The Methodist Service Book* are designed to provide norms for the guidance of the Church, recognizing that Methodism inherited a written liturgy from the Church of England but also developed at an early stage a tradition of 'free' or extempore prayer. The 1974 service reflects the ecumenical convergence that is such a worthy fruit of the Liturgical Movement, though the special relationship to the Church of England is still acknowledged.

The 1990 Methodist Conference agreed to the revision of *The Methodist Service Book*. As far as holy communion is concerned, the provision of alternative eucharistic prayers is a major aim of revision. This not only reflects an ecumenical trend in this country but also of the Methodist Church overseas: for example, the United Methodist Church of the United States of America has prepared some seventy eucharistic prayers to cover both the civil and religious calendar. The Faith and Order Committee is considering the possibility of providing seasonal communion rites as well as standard texts.

However, it should be stated that not all Methodists by any means are happy with the 'given-ness' of the service book or with any kind of 'set rite', especially those who trace their roots to Primitive Methodism or who would define themselves as evangelicals or charismatics. 'Free prayer' remains for them a foundational principle.

The desire on the part of the compilers of *The Methodist Service Book* that the eucharist should be given a more central place within Methodism is evident both by the title of the rite *The Sunday Service* and the statement in the General Directions that:

> 'The worship of the Church is the offering of praise and prayer in which God's Word is read and preached, and in its fullness it includes the Lord's Supper, or Holy Communion.'

The structure of the service is as follows (mandatory sections are marked with an asterisk):

[1] Neil Dixon, 'Towards a New Methodist Service Book', in *Epworth Review*, 17:3, Sept., 1990, p.52.

*The Preparation*

Hymn Collect for purity
Commandments
Confession
Assurance of pardon
* Collect or some other prayer
Hymn or gloria

*The Ministry of the Word*

* Reading: Old Testament, Epistle or both
Hymn
* Gospel
* Sermon
* Intercessions
* Lord's Prayer
Blessing and dismissal of 'those who leave'

*The Lord's Supper*

* The peace
Nicene creed
Hymn
* Bread and wine are brought to the minister or uncovered
* Taking of the bread and wine
* The thanksgiving
* The breaking of the bread
* Silence
Humble access (revised form)
* Invitation to communion
* The communion
* The minister covers the remains
* Silence
* Post-communion prayer
Hymn
Blessing
* Dismissal

There are a number of interesting features. First, in terms of structure, the Methodist compilers followed ecumenical convention in placing the penitential section at the beginning of the rite rather than after the intercessions as in Series 3, the current Church of England form in 1974. The declaration of forgiveness is as follows:

Christ Jesus came into the world to save sinners.
Hear then the word of grace:
Your sins are forgiven.
**Amen. Thanks be to God.**

The declaration is clearly the invoking of a scriptural promise, but by no means all are happy with the second person form, lest there is a hint of a ministerial absolution; 'our' is often substituted. The intercessions are followed by the rather curious dismissal of 'those who leave'. Before the advent of *The Methodist Service Book* there was a widespread tradition of regarding communion as an optional extra after the Preaching Service had finished. The 1975 service, while recognizing that some may wish to leave after the preaching, nevertheless asserts that the Sunday Service with communion is a single service and can claim some credit in reforming previous malpractice. However, as it stands, the dismissal rubric rather contradicts the Methodist insistence that the table of the Lord is open to all and that communion is a 'converting ordinance'. It now reads rather like a piece of liturgical archaeology directed to non-existent catechumens. The Nicene Creed thus becomes the expression of the corporate faith of the eucharistic community rather than the concluding element of the ministry of the word as in the Anglican rites. Humble access becomes a pre-communion devotion and is cast in rather more positive terms than Cranmer's version:

> Lord, we come to your table trusting in your mercy and not in any goodness of our own . . .

As a product of the 1970s, it is not surprising that the eucharistic prayer is reminiscent of Hippolytus. It has the following structure:

> Introductory dialogue
> Preface
> Sanctus and benedictus
> Narrative of institution
> Acclamations
> Anamnesis
> Epiclesis
> Self-offering
> Doxology

The thanksgiving does not include proper prefaces and follows Hippolytus and the 'eastern' shape of the eucharistic prayer in adopting a single epiclesis after the anamnesis rather than the so-called 'split epiclesis' in the Church of England and Roman prayers. The anamnesis is a simple formula in comparison with Rite A:

> Therefore, Father, as he has commanded us,
> we do this in remembrance of him,
> and we ask you to accept our sacrifice of praise and thanksgiving.

Here no attempt is made to define what 'do this' means, nor is the remembrance linked in any particular way to Christ's saving work. While this side-steps some contentious theological issues, it may well be that a fuller statement of the content of the eucharistic *anamnesis* will be required when the service is revised. The fact that the Faith and Order Committee are considering a series of eucharistic prayers suggests that different approaches to the anamnesis will be considered. Indeed the draft seasonal text for Lent and Passiontide reads:

> In obedience to his command
> we recall his suffering and death,
> his resurrection and ascension
> and we look for his coming in glory.
> With these holy gifts
> we offer ourselves
> a single, holy and living sacrifice.

The epiclesis in *The Methodist Service Book* falls short of an explicit invocation of the Spirit; it is rather a petition that the Spirit will be operative in the action of the eucharist. If anything, the weight of the petition falls on the worshippers rather than the elements:

> Grant that by the power of the Holy Spirit we who receive your gifts of bread and wine may share in the body and blood of Christ.

Again, it is likely that revision will provide different forms. The text for Lent/Passiontide include an invocation of the Spirit upon the elements as well as the worshippers:

> Send your Holy Spirit upon us
> and upon these gifts of bread and wine
> that they may be for us
> the body and blood of Christ

A clear invocation upon the elements would be a noteworthy innovation in Methodist liturgy and may be controversial. Some Anglicans share similar concerns about the form of the epiclesis in Eucharistic Prayer B of *Patterns for Worship*. The *MSB* certainly does not have a consecratory formula, bearing witness to the commonly held view that it is the entire eucharistic prayer which effects consecration of the elements rather than a particular formula within it.

**Hymnody**

Any discussion of the place of communion within Methodism must consider the centrality of the hymn book. On a popular level, the hymnal for Methodists is the equivalent of the service book in Anglicanism. And here there is an important difference: whereas the Church of England has never published an authorized hymnal, but relies on private collections, the 'official' Methodist publications are a source of Methodist doctrine. *The Methodist Hymn-Book* of 1933 contained 18 eucharistic hymns out of a collection of 984; in contrast, *Hymns & Psalms* published in 1983 offers at least 38 out of 823. This in itself reflects the greater centrality given to the eucharist in contemporary Methodism, but there is another significant factor. A more developed sacramentalism is evident in the reintroduction of some of John and Charles Wesley's more 'realist' eucharistic teaching. For example, in Charles Wesley's hymn 'Jesus, we thus obey' (MHB 761, H&P 614) the following verses have been reintroduced in *Hymns & Psalms*:

> He bids us drink and eat
> Imperishable food;
> He gives his flesh to be our meat,
> And bids us drink his blood.
>
> Whate'er the Almighty can
> To pardoned sinners give,
> The fullness of our God made man
> We here with Christ receive.[1]

Eucharistic sacrifice is also given expression by incorporating two famous hymns from the catholic tradition of Anglicanism, namely W. C. Dix's 'Alleluia! Sing to Jesus' with the lines

> Thou on earth both priest and victim
> In the eucharistic feast (H&P 592)

and William Bright's 'And now, O Father, mindful of the love' (H&P 593).

[1] This comparison of hymn verses derives from a lecture delivered at St Mary's College, Oscott by the Revd. Dr. S. B. Dawes of The Queen's College, Birmingham.

It is somewhat curious that these Anglican writers should carry the main sacrificial emphasis in the light of the prevalence of sacrificial imagery found in the Wesleys' collection *Hymns on the Lord' Supper* first published in 1745. While evangelical Anglicans recognize an affinity with much of the Wesleys' teaching on grace and conversion, few would be comfortable with this aspect of their sacramental teaching. For example, hymn 4 begins:

O Thou eternal Victim slain
A Sacrifice for guilty Man,
By the Eternal Spirit made
An Offering in the Sinner's stead,
Our everlasting Priest art Thou,
And plead'st thy Death for Sinners now.

Thy Offering still continues New,
Thy Vesture keeps its Bloody Hue,
Thou stand'st the ever slaughtered Lamb,
Thy Priesthood still remains the same,
Thy Years, O God, can never fail, Thy Goodness is unchangeable.

Or the opening verse of 137:

Ye Royal Priests of Jesus, rise
And join the daily Sacrifice,
Join all believers in His Name
And offer up the Spotless Lamb.

The sense here is of a continuing, eternal sacrifice, to which the sacrifice of the church in its eucharistic worship is joined. *Hymns and Psalms* 629 and 554 echo this idea, but the fact that this strand of the Wesleys' teaching is not well represented in the hymns-books may suggest that it is contentious in contemporary Methodism.[1]

*Hymns and Psalms* has, however, included a Charles Wesley hymn which speaks of the role of the Spirit in the eucharistic action:

Come, Holy Ghost, thine influence shed,
  And realize the sign;
Thy life infuse into the bread,
  Thy power into the wine. (MHB 767, H&P 602)

Methodist communion services are marked by their simplicity of style and the fervour of the singing. The tradition of receiving communion 'by tables' i.e. waiting until all the rail has been communicated and dismissed with a blessing by the minister allows space for an unhurried communion. In many ways, a Methodist congregation using the service book is reminiscent of 'low church' Anglican worship; Anglican evangelicals tend to match Methodists in their enjoyment of hearty singing!

[1] See J. E. Rattenbury, *The Eucharistic Hymns of John and Charles Wesley* (Epworth, 1948).

## Presidency

The general directions of 'The Sunday Service' in *The Methodist Service Book* state:

> At the Lord's Supper an ordained Minister, or a layman with a dispensation for the purpose shall preside. Laymen may be invited to share in the Preparation; the Ministry of the Word, including the intercessions; and in the distribution of the bread and wine.

This is not quite the whole story. Standing Order 011 of *The Constitutional Practice and Discipline of the Methodist Church Volume 2* makes provision for lay presidency at the communion where churches through lack of ministers are 'deprived of reasonably frequent and regular celebration of the sacrament of the Lord's Supper.' In practice, this is not invoked very much except for probationer ministers in the period between leaving theological college and ordination to the presbyterate.

Presidency at the holy communion by an ordained Minister is still regarded as a norm in Methodism, but what does such presidency mean? As a response to requests for clarification the 1987 Methodist Conference accepted a report from the Faith and Order Committee stating that the minimum definition of 'presidency' should be that the ordained minister says the whole of the Great Prayer of Thanksgiving. This judgement has proved to be controversial for in some churches it has been the practice to divide the eucharistic prayer among two or three voices, the narrative of the institution alone being reserved for the minister. In spite of the ruling by Conference it is likely that pluriform practice will continue.

## Children and Communion

The 1987 Methodist Conference approved a set of guidelines drawn up by the Division of Education and Youth on the place of!children at holy communion.[1] The Conference report on Christian Initiation in 1985 concluded:

> Baptism is the one essential rite for entry into the Church and those who have received it are entitled to their place at the Lord's Table, though it may be expedient for this to be delayed.

While wholeheartedly welcoming the statement on baptism, the last ten words are to be regretted. In the end, the guidelines leave the issue in the hands of each individual Church Council but the issue of admission to communion on baptism and therefore infant communion is somewhat fudged. For example, guidelines C and D read:

> The Church Council should satisfy itself that the child shows an awareness of the significance of the Lord's Supper, and the faith response appropriate to the child's age and experience.
>
> The Church has a responsibility to discriminate and test, but this must not become the opportunity for adults to deprive children of the means of grace simply because they are children.

This would rule out infant communion and makes some form of understanding the basis for admission not baptism. At least Methodism is free from any link between confirmation and admission to communion, but we regret that aspects of the report which assert the significance of baptism are undermined by the insistence that some form of understanding is essential.

[1] See *Children at Holy Communion: Guidelines* (Methodist Church Division of Education and Youth, 1987).

## 5. HOLY COMMUNION IN THE URC

The URC includes traditions which write non-prescriptive liturgy. Thus ministers have the freedom to compose their own material, including eucharistic prayers. With this in mind, we will first look at the structure of the service, making some preliminary comments about the whole rite. Then we look in more depth at some particular theological issues.

A. THE URC ORDER

### 1 Structure

| ***A Book of Services* 1980** | ***Service Book* 1989** |
|---|---|
| *The word and the prayers* | |
| Sentence | Sentence |
| Prayer of approach and hymn | Prayer of approach |
| Confession of sin | Confession of sin |
| Assurance of pardon | Assurance of pardon |
| Gloria or kyries | Kyries and gloria |
| Prayer for grace | Prayer for grace |
| | *The Ministry of the word* |
| Lessons hymns and sermon | Lessons, hymns and sermon |
| Creed, hymn, notices | Creed, notices |
| Prayers | Intercessions |
| *The Thanksgiving and the Communion* | *The Sacrament of the Lord's Supper* |
| Invitation and gracious words | Invitation |
| The peace | |
| Offertory and hymn | Offertory |
| Narrative of institution | Narrative of institution |
| Taking | |
| The thanksgiving | The thanksgiving |
| Lord's prayer | Lord's prayer |
| | The peace |
| Breaking | Breaking and pouring |
| | Agnus dei |
| Sharing the bread and the wine | Sharing the bread and wine |
| Acclamation | |
| Prayer, hymn or doxology | Prayer, nunc dimittis, praise |
| Dismissal and blessing | Dismissal and blessing |

A second Order of Worship in the 1989 book reflects the tradition of the Churches of Christ. For brevity we concentrate on the first Order.

Both URC books and the *ASB* share a common structure. However, at some points there are significant differences. The URC books have no text of the Nicene Creed within the rite. Both books have them at the back, but in practice they are rarely used, and may be unfamiliar to the church member. Also the peace has moved from the position in the 1980 book shared with the *ASB* (at the start of the ministry of the sacrament) to the Roman position in the 1989 book (after the Lord's Prayer). It is unclear how this expresses Reformed tradition, and is certainly not the most ancient place.

**2 Language**
The 1989 *Service Book* has three new eucharistic prayers in the first order. The first with its long section on the exodus—wilderness—promised land story in the preface expresses a liberation theology outlook and it is based on the San Miguelito Liturgy from Panama. In light of the explicit reference to inclusive language in the preface to the book, it is surprising that there is not more use of 'feminine' images of God both in the eucharistic prayer and in the rest of the book. This contrasts with *Patterns for Worship* in which Rite C includes the Biblical phrase 'as a mother tenderly gathers her children you embraced people as your own' in Eucharistic Prayer B.

**3 Presidency**
Unlike the *ASB*, the *Service Book* does not say who is allowed to preside at various points in the service. Usually this would be an ordained minister of word and sacrament. It is however possible, in exceptional circumstances, for someone with recognised status in the congregation to be authorized by the District Synod to preside. This would often be a lay preacher or an elder. In practice too, some ministers may preside by inviting lay people to give thanks for the bread and for the wine. But the general effect of the union of Congregationalism and Presbyterianism has been to place greater restrictions on lay presidency.

**4 Children and Communion**
The traditional practice of the churches forming the URC is that becoming a member (confirmation) was the gateway to communion. This might even have been talked about in the language of 'joining the church'. This would often have occurred when candidates were in their late teens or as young adults. This church like many others has been rethinking its traditional pattern, leaving a great variety of practice. Some congregations will follow a traditional pattern. Others have a local policy of giving communion to children. This depends on the minister, the elders and the Church Meeting who develop the local policy. The general policy of the denomination being to allow diversity of practice.

B. THEOLOGICAL ISSUES

**1 The Assurance of Pardon**
The Assurance of Pardon is clearly of a declaratory nature. Based on, or using, Scripture, sins are declared forgiven. 'To all who turn to him he Jesus says: 'Your sins are forgiven' . . . 'or "God grants you the forgiveness of sins".' This seems to do what *The Book of Common Prayer* wanted but could not quite bring itself to say in the absolution at Morning and Evening Prayer. However, it differs from the Anglican approach in the *BCP* communion absolution, developed in the ablutions of the *ASB*. 'Almighty God, who forgives all who truly repent, have mercy upon you . . . through Jesus Christ our Lord, Amen.' is a most subtle prayer. Grammatically it is an optative subjunctive; it expresses a wish. But the force of the prayer is that it is an event in which God forgives sins. This is externalized in some circles by people crossing themselves. The URC has gone for a clear declaration of forgiveness: 'Your sins are forgiven'; 'God grants you the forgiveness of your sins'. The danger of declarations of forgiveness is that they come

perilously close to having the same effect as the medieval *ego te absolvo*, of placing the minister as the mediator of forgiveness. Perhaps optative subjunctives have more to commend them than at first appears.

**2 Offertory**

The 1980 book envisages a monetary collection (called the offerings) and an offertory procession of the bread and the wine. The prayer is then said:

> 'Eternal God, we come with these gifts to offer our sacrifice of praise and the service of our lives; through Jesus Christ our Lord.'

This is developed in the 1989 book to include the possibility of the use of the Roman offertory prayers with the addition of:

> Blessed are you, Lord of all creation,
> Through your goodness we have ourselves to offer,
> fruit of the womb, and formed by your love.
> We will become your people for the world.
> **Blessed be God for ever**.

The Roman Catholic prayers are proving to be remarkably popular, and arguably had heard more commonly outside Roman Catholicism than in, for in the mass they are often said quietly by the priest during the hymn. Perhaps there is a feeling that something needs to be said to set aside the elements. But would not that be the function of words of taking? Such offertory prayers are pre-emptive of the eucharistic prayer, a thanksgiving before the great thanksgiving, and need reconsideration.

Gregory Dix saw the offertory (of the elements) as the first of the actions of the eucharist. This has been attacked by Colin Buchanan[1] and the *ASB* clearly distinguished the placing of the elements on the table (section 32), the collection (section 34), and the taking of the bread (section 36). The 1980 URC book had a separate taking but this has dropped out of the 1989 book. A solemn entrance of the elements is found in the Presbyterian tradition, *The Book of Common Order* of the Church of Scotland even calling it a Great Entrance. This is in part through the influence of the Church Service Society in the 1867 *Euchologion*, the beginning of liturgical renewal in the Church of Scotland. But there are older traditions of a solemn entrance of the elements going back to the Westminster Divines. A distinctive feature of the latest URC book is its importation of prayers from a variety of traditions. But at this point has the caution of the Reformation over oblation been forgotten? If 'offertory prayers' are to be included, might not those of the Lima Liturgy better express Reformed theology?

**3 The position of the Narrative of Institution**

Anglicans are used to the narrative being the central part of the eucharistic prayer. To many in the URC this might be an innovation. There is a strong tradition of reading the narrative as a warrant and then having a thanksgiving without the narrative. The *Westminster Directory* envisages this pattern of service but in no respect sees this as undermining consecration. It talks of 'those elements, otherwise common, are now set apart and

[1] C. O. Buchanan, *The End of the Offertory* (Grove Liturgical Studies No 14, Grove Books, 1978)

sanctified to this holy use, by the word of Institution and Prayer.' After the thanksgiving it says 'The Elements being now sanctified by the Word and Prayer'. The theology of consecration therefore rests on the words in 1 Timothy 4.4-5; 'everything God created is good, and nothing is to be rejected if it is received with thanksgiving, because it is consecrated by the word of God and prayer'. The Puritans did not want to reject the consecration of the elements, rather they wanted to disagree with the Catholics as to how that came about and what effect it had.

The narrative is regarded as necessary. It would be against the tradition of the URC to have a communion without the narrative at all. But the relation of the narrative and the eucharistic prayer is variable. Its position can be either before (as a warrant), in the prayer (as the *ASB*), or after it (at the fraction). The 1989 book has the narrative, not printed in one, bracketed in another, and included in the third. Clearly it is not regarded as necessary within the eucharistic prayer.

Bryan Spinks has questioned Anglicans, asking whether they would be prepared to use a eucharistic prayer without a narrative.[1] The Eastern examples of prayers with only partial references to the last supper or without narratives at all, not least the ancient Addai and Mari, seem to rest on a consecration effected by the Holy Spirit, as is expressed in the epiclesis.[2] *The Book of Common Prayer* would seem to continue the medieval theory of consecration through the recital of the narrative of institution by the priest. The *ASB* however has turned to the theory that the consecration is by thanksgiving and the whole eucharistic prayer is consecratory, not any particular part. What is important to realize that there different theologies of consecration underlying and within the different liturgical traditions.

### 4 'Pleading his eternal sacrifice'

This small phrase in the anamnesis of Thanksgiving I in the 1989 book has been of some debate both in the URC and in contemporary Anglicanism. The eucharistic prayer continues after the acclamations:

> Therefore remembering the work and passion
> of our Saviour Christ
> and pleading his eternal sacrifice,
> we set forth this memorial
> which he willed us to make.

What exactly does this phrase mean? There are two issues. First, in what way do we plead Christ's sacrifice? Second, what is the meaning of the phrase 'eternal sacrifice'?

J. M. Barkley sees the pleading of the sacrifice to be deep in the Reformed tradition.[3] The eucharist is a renewal of the covenant inaugurated by

[1] B. Spinks, 'The Institution Narrative in the Eucharistic Prayer' in *News of Liturgy*, no 157, (Jan 1988), pp 2-4.
[2] T. Mannooramparampil, 'Epiclesis in the Anaphora of Addai and Mari', in *Christian Orient*, Vol IX no 2-3, (June-September, 1988), pp.134-147.
[3] J. M. Barkley, 'Pleading His Eternal Sacrifice', in B. D. Spinks (ed), *The Sacrifice of Praise* (CVL, 1981) pp.123-140.

Christ on the cross. As mediator, Christ is in heaven interceding for us and in the eucharist eternal grace is revealed and renewed. Our unworthy prayer is based on Christ alone, hence we plead his sacrifice. So Watts was able to talk in his hymns of pleading Christ's blood, and pleading has a long history in the post-Reformation discussion of being used by both Calvinist and evangelical traditions. Perhaps equally important it was used by the Archbishops in their defence of Anglican Orders in 1897.

Questions have been asked of the phrase 'eternal sacrifice' whether this expresses the Reformed view. J. M. Todd said of this phrase commenting on the first thanksgiving in *A Book of Services* 1980:

> 'We have preferred "perfect sacrifice" to "eternal sacrifice" used in the Book of Common Order ("pleading his eternal sacrifice") as being more scriptural and, we venture to think, theologically more defensible. Christ offered a perfect sacrifice on the Cross once for all: that is what we celebrate. It has eternal significance; but is more accurately described as "perfect" than as an "eternal" sacrifice.'[1]

Therefore the 1980 prayer said;

> Holy Lord God,
> by what we do here
> in remembrance of Christ
> we celebrate his perfect sacrifice on the Cross
> and declare his glorious resurrection and ascension;

Neither 'pleading' nor 'an eternal sacrifice' were acceptable here.

*Patterns for Worship* has developed in a slightly different direction. Alternative eucharistic prayer B says:

> Father, as we plead with confidence his sacrifice made once for all,
> we remember his dying and rising in glory,
> and we rejoice that he prays for us at your right hand:

In this prayer we find the sacrifice has been made 'once for all'. Maybe the phrase 'eternal sacrifice' is seen as too ambiguous; suggesting to some that the sacrifice is still continuing in eternity. It may therefore be a shock to some to read in Calvin:

> 'the blood of Christ is not corrupted by any decay but flows continually in unadulterated purity, it will suffice for us to the end of the world . . .
> 'Christ who rose from the dead to give us life pours his own life into us. 'This is the continual consecration of his life that the blood of Christ is continually being shed before the face of the Father to spread over heaven and earth.'

This Reformed language would probably be contrary to much contemporary evangelical Anglican thinking.

### 5 Invoking the Holy Spirit

Calvin had a strong role for the Holy Spirit in his eucharistic theology. While the Prayer of Consecration in the 1662 *BCP* is silent about the Holy

[1] J. M. Todd, 'Tradition and Change: Worship in the United Reformed Church' in *Liturgical Review*, Vol 5 No 1, (1975), p.14.

Spirit, the *Westminster Directory* was more explicit. The Thanksgiving was to be to this effect:

> 'pray to God . . . to vouchsafe his gracious presence, and the effectual working of his Spirit in us, and so to sanctify these Elements . . . that we may receive by faith the Body and Blood of Jesus Christ . . . and so to feed on him.'

The URC continues to follow this advice.

Evangelical Anglicans have tended to be cautious about the epiclesis. There has been suspicion about blessing objects, e.g. wedding rings or baptismal water, and caution about invoking the Spirit upon the eucharistic elements. The *ASB* Eucharistic Prayers seem to have been written with this in mind. 'Grant that by the power of your Holy Spirit these gifts of bread and wine may be to us his body and blood.' The two words 'to us' may appear insignificant, but they are of help to some consciences by seeming to soften the epiclesis. Yet this may be a delusion, for the same form of expression is found in the second eucharistic prayer of the Roman Missal.

In the tradition of the *Westminster Directory* and of recent Presbyterianism, the URC has much stronger invocations on the elements than the *ASB*. Thanksgiving III reads:

> Lord, send on us and on this thanksgiving meal the Spirit of Life,

and in the Second Order:

> By your Holy Spirit sanctify us and these your gifts of bread and wine . . .

Although there are other less directly consecratory invocations in the other prayers, there is a strong tradition of invocation of the Spirit upon both the people and the elements in the Reformed Churches.

## 6. ECUMENISM AND THE FUTURE

This booklet has taken an Anglican look at selected services from two Free Churches. For the purpose of simplification a three-way comparison of the issues has not been attempted. But it is hoped that such a comparison has been stimulated while reading. Looking at a broader context we can now ask the question: as Anglicans what do we learn? Also we venture to make some suggestions for the future.

### Growth Together

The round of liturgical revision that produced *The Methodist Service Book, A Book of Services,* and *The Alternative Service Book* was much influenced by the Liturgical Movement. This emphasised the influence of patristic liturgies, the centrality of the eucharist and the importance of participation. The result is that the services of the three churches, and particularly eucharistic worship, look very similar. What differences would an outsider find in say a Methodist and Anglican communion? They may well say that they are almost the same.

This is the fruit of a more ecumenically minded approach to liturgical study. It is no longer appropriate to study the liturgy of one's denomination in isolation. Indeed ecumenical co-operation in parishes is making knowledge of other traditions essential. The Joint Liturgical Group (JLG) also has been of influence. The two-year lectionary has been adopted by all three denominations. Their work on the Office and Holy Week has been of value and Anglican clergy may well find Free Church ministers who are liturgically minded and who use this material.

This is leading to a change in the traditional battle lines. Anglicans may be pushing for a baptistry in an LEP, and Free Church ministers arguing for the common cup. Anglicans have been widely influenced by the charismatic movement, and so testimony and open prayer may be embraced in services. Indeed the 'Family Service' movement cuts across the denominations and *Patterns for Worship* may allow even greater freedom in Anglican worship. The churches are changing and a new round of liturgical revision is in the air. Anglicans are beginning to think about the year 2000 when the *ASB* authorization runs out. The new URC *Service Book* is here and may suggest a new more pastorally orientated direction in the future.

### Still separated!

There has however been a long history of the failure of Churches to unite. The Church of England and Methodist Church unity scheme failed. Then Covenanting for Unity aborted (except in Wales). The URC unions have been the best example of a growth towards denominational unity. Now the Methodist Church and the URC are beginning to explore the possibility of union. If the national schemes involving Anglicans have failed, then locally there is more hope. Local covenants proliferate, and LEPs continue to flourish. Indeed there are reported to be 600 LEPs now in England.

In this climate of unity, joint worship together is happening. What is surprising is that more ecumenical rites have not developed. The contrast